This Fool's Journey
Through Tarot's 22 Major Arcana

By
Melanie Gendron
CREATOR OF *THE GENDRON TAROT*

BLUE LIGHT PRESS • 1ST WORLD LIBRARY

1ST WORLD
PUBLISHING

SAN FRANCISCO • FAIRFIELD • DELHI

This Fool's Journey
Through Tarot's 22 Major Arcana
Copyright ©2014 By Melanie Gendron

For information contact:

1st World Publishing
PO Box 2211
Fairfield, Iowa 52556
www.1stworldpublishing.com

Blue Light Press
www.bluelightpress.com
Email: bluelightpress@aol.com

Cover, Illustrations, Book Design:
Melanie Gendron

Website:
www.MelanieGendron.com

First Edition

ISBN 9781421886794

Library of Congress Control Number: 2013920750

Acknowledgments

"The Fool's Passage", "Gypsy" and "Now" poems appear in *The Gendron Tarot* book, U.S. Games Systems, Inc., 2004

The following appeared in *The Connection Magazine*, www.ConnectionMagazineOnline.com: "On Awaking: Gratitude" (January, 2013), "Angels Are Real" (September, 2013), "All Souls' Hallowed Day" (October, 2013)

Thank You

I am filled with gratitude
for all the relationships and
experiences that inspired this book.

Special thanks to:
Reverend Agatha for motherly guidance,
Cassandra for being a great daughter,
Steve for his supportive friendship,
Elizabeth Porter for editing,
Diane Frank and Rodney Charles
for helping to make this book possible,
and to all who have inspired me to get real.

Table of Contents

DEDICATION

For Reverend Agatha,
who when I complained,
would say repeatedly,
It's your own picture show.

She inspired me
to ask my mirror,
Who am I, after all.

Preface

About Face—It's time to face one's Self.

In this, my twilight time, I reflect upon the world, and wonder how I made it this far—stumbling, a once overly idealistic youth, believing the dreams I projected and then, rejected.

In a still, quiet space, I contemplate my life's passage, both joyful and sorrowful. Suffice it to say, life happens, and things have not turned out exactly as I thought they would.

I was born on a twenty-second day, with a birth date numerology of nine, which is an invitation to a life of self mastery, completion, and the challenges a desire for perfection attracts. I am naturally drawn to Tarot's 22 major arcana, specifically IX The Hermit, a card often associated with teachers and mystics. The Hermit's deepest meaning is *Enlightened Being*. I know the quest for enlightenment has certainly defined my being.

This book evolved from a desire to reveal, understand, accept and love myself more. Because we weave the fabric of our world together, and being a number nine, I also want to share my thoughts and insights, hoping that it may be expansive for you as well. Though on myriad paths, we are on this earth walk together.

The goddess Quan Yin, a Bodhisattva of immeasurable compassion, inspires this process of Self discovery—to cultivate fulfillment through mindful self-awareness, self-forgiveness, self-acceptance and the unconditional love experienced with surrender to the power of our Higher Self as we awaken to the one source of life we share.

Each one of us is a divine Fool seeking our own spiritual path to transcend time. We search for validation from others, and truth seems illusive until we traverse the gulf between ego and simply Being.

The stories we weave on the spiraling path home can secure wisdom and disclose our true nature. Whether or not we are present, in process of digesting memory, or projecting our future, what we perceive becomes real. In every one of us, there is at least one book about our lives, with various conclusions based on perceptual reality.

Shared stories tell us we are not alone as we see others confronted with similar life challenges. We are inspired by sagas of overcoming obstacles and revealing human potential; they remind us we are at choice no matter the appearance.

Ancient wisdom teaches that consciousness structures knowledge, and our state of awareness determines how we act. Born to pristine ignorance, we become aware through the fundamental urge to discover. The desire to become all we can be appears coded in our DNA.

Accessing the unconscious for clarity through daily journal writing has been a life saver for me: it is something I highly recommend. Articles, poems, stories and revelations flow forth with the intent to be authentic.

This book spans years of writing sessions, intimately sharing my life perceptions and experiences relative to Tarot's 22 major arcana. I have found these universal archetypes provide a map of consciousness that reflects absolute truth, the quintessential eternal wisdom gained through conscientious awareness.

An example of my seeking to embody the cosmic principles inherent in Tarot, I hope *This Fool's Journey* will inspire you, or at the very least, entertain and stir your imagination.

Welcome to my mind;
may it speak yours as well.
Welcome to my heart;
may we both grow for sharing.
Melanie

The Fool's Passage

Heaven's own has now begun the journey,
Life to choose a path to Life.
Magical dancer of *above / below*,
With tools to create a world,
Seeks the hidden wisdom of True Self
To reprogram patterns of lack.

The disciplined Mind invites authority and power.
Respectful of tradition, it remains open to discover
Unity, Love and Balance in the play of opposites.
Overcoming obstacles, the Soul is victoriously
Expressive of Divine Force.
Illumined, the throes of fortune do not bind.

Equanimity releases suffering,
Effecting a complete change of perspective.
The Soul reborn tempers through Spirit
To reveal Shadow and make a choice—
Love or Fear, to be free or not, block or flow,
Crumble or Phoenix rise.

Stars shine bright in the darkest sky
To inspire the Fool's sight
Beyond illusion's wall to Truth.
Having attained Light through atonement,
The journey completes in wholeness,
For one is meant to be as One.

South

Wands ◆ Fire
Intent ◆ Innocence
Choices ◆ Karma

1 Am

Like moths,
from the abyss
toward the light
we come.

Emerging,
limbs of a tree,
cries urge a drink
of mother's milk—

Bone, sinew, blood,
full stomach birth
from the loam that
rests perpetual
beneath the earth.

Grave brevity
invites Spring.

O
The Fool

This is the first day of the rest of my life.

+ Choice • Beginnings • Innocence

‑ Immature • Reckless • Folly

The Fool

I am at choice, with everywhere to go.

On the verge of incarnation, I stand ready to live—Spirit become manifest duality, forming experience by choice.

Uranus, the idealist, inspires evolutionary thought to liberate my soul.

Gifted this journey, I am a divine Fool who initiates life awareness and unfolds consciousness to support the passage.

In this waking dream of infinite possibility, could I be experiencing lucid REM sleep in a lab experiment, or acting improvisation on an imagined stage in a make-believe universe?

Getting into the part, I could become the dream.

BIRTH

Womb floating,
fear a first emotion,
foetus anxiety fed—

I leapt.

Tight contractions down
the dark wet tunnel
into a scream of light,

Hands greeted me
and I forgot.

Being touched
felt safe.

Joy

Joy floods my veins
like effervescent ginger ale,
and I marvel at how much
I have come to love me.

I invite happiness,
an ocean soft breeze,
to embody
what I choose.

A brave fool with heart
to leap the void,
I embrace truth
as a beacon of Light.

Love's sanctuary
intends a life that
transcends the suffering
of separation.

1
The Magus

What you see is what you get.

+ Individuality • Magic • Manifestation

- Ego Attachment • Greed

The Magus

I am a magician creating a magical life.

Wand of Fire, Cup of Water, Pentacle of Earth, and Sword of Air, I call upon you to manage nature's tendencies and experiences that I may master life.

WAND

Identify the challenge, enhance concentration
and provide solution.

CUP

Shape experience with creativity and imagination.

SWORD

Initiate action.

PENTACLE

Grant the fruit of my actions.

Thank You.

Beginning Life Mastery 101

After Mama and Papa died . . .
I made no waves,
fearing to be a state ward
like my cousin.

I longed for family,
a reason to be alive,
things to do, people to please,
the sound of parental praise . . .

Aspiring to perfection,
insecure, I wondered
if I had been seeded
to the wrong planet.

When would the
Mother Ship
rescue
me?

In Search of I Am

Sensually alive, idealizing absolutes
I persevere—persist—perpetuate
darkness
to illumine a way Home.

Between remembrance and not yet
I bear perceptual
witness
to the Power that heals pain.

Nurtured in a sea of silence,
held by loving arms,
confident
that I am loved and loving,

I invite presence, the gift of Now,
an eternal instant of
appreciation
with the grace to become.

11

The High Priestess

Still waters run deep.

+ Hidden Wisdom • Subconscious

‑ Superficial

The High Priestess

Listening to my inner voice, I come to know.

Guardian of the Akashic Records, a storehouse of individual and universal knowledge—I am the High Priestess with perfect memory that continuously records all occurrence throughout time, neutral, transcending conscious consent or judgment.

Moon reflective, cosmic and mysterious,
all forms perceptible to human senses
evolve from mental energy
transmitting from the level
of subconscious
Self.

People say one thing,
then do another.
It makes little sense
on the periphery of
unknown.

I say,

*Listen
to know
and reveal
your Truth.*

Who Is This Person?

Who is this person who stares back
too real to comprehend?

A reflective image of purple hue, sensing
Genesis has a perfect world ahead.

I know.
I believe in miracles.

The day invariably follows night,
Sun's dependence a law.

Love is divine foundation,
eternal, transcending ebb and flow.

It redesigns form as it reforms,
renews and reaffirms wholeness.

I look into ocean deep eyes,
reflecting a universe.

Questing, found and profound,
I am almost too real
to comprehend.

W/hole

I have a hole in me

it breathes lonely
aches
longs
yearns
desires
precipitates change
procures life
hungers more
seeks
journeys
circles
river to ocean
travels

when we met
it drew you in

my womb
spiraled wholly
expanding my child

III

The Empress

Mother is at Home.

+ Abundance • Fertility • Fruitfulness

− Infertility • Lack

The Empress

Consider the lilies of the field, how they grow;
they toil not, neither do they spin:
And yet I say unto you,
that even Solomon in all his glory
was not arrayed like one of these.
—Mathew 6:28-29, Holy Bible

I am the creative essence that issues forth abundance—global thought, forever, timeless, imaginative, a Great Mother who creates the material world and sustains nature, both receiving and giving, an eternal pregnancy in anticipation of idea.

One and two combined
unite one and duality,
creating something more
than either alone.

Beauty equals love,
and Venus has
a secret door
to knowing.

It invites you
to enter.

Mama Was a Shaman

She made irresistible treats on a wood stove.
Her abundant breasts matched her gifts,
the smell of fresh baked bread,
pies and Thanksgiving.

A shaman with healing arts
from her Native American roots,
she even knew the day she would die,
which happened when I was ten.

After, she visited during a tense night.
I was a young mother unable to sleep,
abandoned, having taken too many pills . . .
thick tongue in my mouth, floating off-world.

Mama's spirit held me in the dark tunnel,
soothing my angst like a warm sun.
She died with a promise to
come back and prove eternity.

I had waited for years.

DIVING

1

He said, "It's like being in your mother's womb," and the words reverberated like a mantra. My ears wouldn't clear; I feared drowning, and the suit felt claustrophobic.

Kneeling on the pool bottom to practice mask clearing, the instructor removed his mask and blew air through his nose with bubbles dancing around his face and upward to the surface. It was a catatonic moment—he was so beautiful, an image of birth and becoming—that I could not move.

Simultaneously, I felt the pressure of water on my head, ears blocked, humming anxiety. I surfaced quickly, unsure of my diving potential. Sensing death while witnessing life, I felt painfully separate from mother's womb.

2

Movement of
Ocean
Teaches
Happiness
Enlightenment
Reality

The waves moved in like her love, given and retrieved, promises made and broken, reflections of inconstancy. They moved like my love, held back in judgment, a reflection of fear. She was the unknown, changing from clouds to sun instantly.

It took me years to discover it wasn't mother or me, but the hostile world raining on her sensitivity. It took even longer to see patterns and the agreement to create the world we shared.

I saw her as imperfect, made excuses for her weakness. A perfect master, she ignited my longing for more.

I couldn't fathom how to deal with her crises, so went about seeking my own path. Eventually, all I saw in mother, I saw in me.

3

The sea was calm with sun reflecting off gentle caps as we jumped waves. Everyone seemed so light and friendly. Whales appeared on the horizon, jetting diamond water, then gone.

We dropped anchor off Molokini Island as I prepared for my first deep ocean dive. Visibility was prime, over 100 feet. First in, I snorkeled to the descent line and waited for the group while entranced by the world below. I descended slowly, diatoms reflecting sunlight, translucent stars of nutrient. Bubbles danced with the light higher and higher as I embraced the depths.

Wordless, timeless, unlimited space, no questions asked or needed . . . the ocean held me suspended. Fish moved continually in a perpetual variety of creation.

4

I was at Home.

WE FEAR . . .

We fear our power,
and rightly so—until ego is tamed.
Once aligned with our true nature,
we can release the illusion of *mine*
inherent in craving dominion
over the world we create.

IV
The Emperor

We are infinitely powerful.

+ **AUTHORITY • DISCIPLINE • POWER**
- **UNDISCIPLINED CHARACTER**

The Emperor

I am the progenitor of an empire.

I, The Emperor, provide a perfect balance for The Empress. She guides the right or global side of the brain while I govern the left or linear side. I add reason to her compassion with my definitive mentality that regulates, supervises, classifies and discriminates.

Protector of life by command and power, my counsel always helps to overcome obstacles or avoid danger, transforming adverse into friendly circumstance. I am Mars to The Empress' Venus, and our complimentary energies are strongly defined.

Think of me as both square and cube, symbols for the physical plane and concrete things. Equal sides imply perfect order, providing boundaries to define form. The circle, representative of The Empress, has no beginning or end, lacking definition. I apply linear thought to interpret eternity.

I am the thought that gestates in the womb of becoming.

PAPA

He would talk about traveling the world during his years at sea. Enraptured, I envisioned the wondrous places he had seen, and being there with him.

He would fish in a rowboat where girls were not allowed. I remember watching and waiting like a woman whose mate is at sea.

A fireman who lived at the firehouse except on his days off, he would come home and curse Mama.

I figured that when I grew up . . . I could marry Papa and make him happy.

I didn't know Mama loved Papa until he was dying.

Then, they sat long, quiet hours in the kitchen just holding hands.

Sweat Lodge

I showered, entering the sweat lodge where drums swirled oppressive heat into my lungs. I lay on the floor for cooler air, and settled into the repetitive beat, ready to attract some animal allies.

I entered a tunnel—circular, ridged, yet fluidly smooth— and moved effortlessly, twisting through the earth. An otter appeared, presenting himself in various postures. Coy, he did not answer when I asked if he would return with me.

Then, a red fox eagerly upstaged Otter, whirling us around, hand in paw, while Otter banged a drum against his belly. Fox agreed to return, but Otter enjoyed his tease until he said we could hold hands for the trip back.

I was to dance each and be recognized to secure their help. The drums played a fast roll; and circling, we traveled back rapidly through the tunnel.

Agatha, Gail and I enjoyed cooler air in the shower room as candlelight flickered, and music inspired a dance. I fluffed a fox tail becoming four-legged with reflections flickering on the wall.

Gail, whose totem is Fox, expressed her recognition.

I ran outside to the pool. My inner otter dove in fast from the deep side into perfectly tepid, silky water. I could barely contain myself rolling around, playing with a ball that floated on the surface. Women nearby laughed.

Agatha dove in, and said, *You're an otter!*

A Later Dive at Point Lobos . . .

We rode out to sea, pristine air licking the glass surface, and he was there resting in the kelp. My delight sang out, *Dear Otter, I am so happy to see you!*

He looked into my eyes, clapping his hands as he broke loose from the kelp, rolling in the water, joy apparent. I remembered the outrageous aliveness my otter swim invoked.

Our first dive was in Bluefish Cove at ninety feet. With ears slow to acclimate, I have indulged gradual descents, enjoying the bubbles rising with fluorescent rainbows toward the surface.

Glancing upward, I saw kelp silhouetted against brilliant light streaming down like God sending illumination to a waiting Earth.

Later, I danced clever Fox and playful Otter to chants, flute and drum; and the depth of their gifts were revealed. They helped channel healing purification so joy could become a palpable reality.

After many hours of aloneness, loneliness dissolved, for we were silent together—

And empowered.

GREAT FATHER

Great Father
That is All in all,
I accept my inheritance
with humility,
knowing that I Am
Your divine expression.

I bask in
Your warm kindness,
Your infinite mercy,
Your unlimited gift.

Though I stumble,
Your hands will
lift me up.

V
The Heirophant

Show me the way . . .

+ TRADITION • DOGMA

- NON-CONFORMIST • UNORTHODOX

The Heirophant

We have heard the call to faith . . .

Expressing a triumphant and eternal intelligence, I represent the foundation of all dogmas, the Universal Principle that remains constant, true and uncorrupted.

Taurian, I resist change,
more secure and comfortable
with traditional belief systems.

Verily I declare . . .
Five is the middle path between one and nine.
Human beings mediate Divine Will and nature.

I amplify the divine voice in humankind by
managing the sense of hearing, especially
the subtle hearing that intuits one's inner deity.

Hear me, for I Am the way.

Now

Desire and Logos
One
thought of union.

Gloriously graced,
each act, every touch
in hand with Unity.

A clear path marks
the way Home; yet each
must find it alone.

Remember—separation
never existed except for
thinking it.

Days of Longing

The days of longing
are too long,
much less the time
we spend together.

Yet memories crowd
while mind, body, spirit
ache between
separation and unity.

Resurrected,
moments of connection
are all there is
of value.

We never quite arrive
until we stop running . . .
what is there to avoid
when only love matters?

VI
The Lovers

Mars & Venus, Shiva & Shakti, Yin & Yang
Balance is the name of the game . . .

+ HARMONIOUS CHOICE • LOVE • TRUST

- INSECURITY • SEPARATION

The Lovers

Love alleviates the lonely heart and
spreads the light of hope, joy and compassion.

Lovers, the celestial essence of Archangel Raphael, Healer of God, has graced each of us with his beneficially regenerative energy.

Fertility results naturally when both yin and yang function in harmony, cultivating the fruit of one's inner marriage, the wholeness of an integrated personality. As we relate wholeheartedly, we gain in wholeness of Being.

In conscious relationship, mates serve as mirrors to each other, reflecting love and placing attention on synchronistic relationship, ideally gaining command of emotional display.

A balanced lover guides the sorting of information, ideas and feelings to arrive at optimal decisions. Disposing the extraneous, the heart and mind unite with clarity to enable wise, caring action. Through forgiveness, anger dissolves and harmony flourishes.

Lovers encourage peace and resolution with the intent to grow perfect love—no matter the challenge—rising from the ashes many times to love again.

THE INNER MARRIAGE FIRST
for oneself to share
One Whole Self

The Long Dark

The ghost of
what might have been
beckoned like
a long-lost friend

It brought winter,
holding my heart
in an icy tomb
to protect the
remnants of love.

From the briar patch,
I could hide
and witness
life eat life
rabbit wise,

a pioneer
circling wagons,
under attack
with paradise
just a mirage . . .

Yet in my vision
I am not alone—
an old couple weeding,
years of roses
between us.

We Could

We would not question
our bodies' passion for
timeless dancing.
Mountain high we could
gaze upon the valley
like birds about to soar.

We might hike the hills and
picnic through long shadows.
We could tent overnight
by a trickling stream
and listen to coyotes
bay the moon.

We could do it . . .
change our lives if we choose
to hear creation's hum—
in communion, at
once in our lifetimes'
synchronicity.

The energy is ours to use,
the why to know,
the choice to choose . . .

If we listen, we may hear
the secret that tells us
how to love.

WEST

Water ◆ Cups
Emotion ◆ Introspection
Subconscious ◆ Desire

Gypsy

Many voices chatter
the great dark horse rears
his hooves to strike them quiet
dust and sneeze a whinny to his stall

I would ride him to center in magic
wood breaking either side
leaves licking face
sounding an earth echoed gallop

A wild scream
could curb the ache
the cry an inside whimper
made in longing

Vast asleep my gypsy glides
dream of stallion
rides the night
forest deep she draws the reins

VII
The Chariot

Take Charge!

+ Control • Victory

- Out of Control

The Chariot

The early bird gets the worm!

Transcending the limitations of ignorance, I choose right action spontaneously by centering in absolute, true Self consciousness. Joy is my motivating mantra.

Divine guidance protects a Self-reliant soul willing to listen; therefore, I am evolving dominion over senses, emotions and desires. Emotional stability invites victory—consequently, I have developed a basic working relationship with three levels of being:

Subconscious,
Self-conscious,
and Super-conscious.

Powered by the interconnections of microcosm and macrocosm, I am a universal individual recognizing the body, or chariot, as a vehicle of deified work on earth. The charioteer, my personality, defers to higher, authentic Self-functioning to drive the Chariot.

Stepping beyond the sheltered world, I greet life from an expanded perspective, increasing dependence on the inner Self rather than being at the affect of external circumstance.

Knowing one is the vehicle through which Divinity moves encourages a victorious life experience.

Angels Are Real

The angel said, *In this realm of all potential, angelic forces offer guidance to one who asks. Answers are within every question, and the way to fulfillment begins with emotive desire. Free will drives the chariot of want to a destiny of choice; as one wills, so does one receive.*

"I understand," said I, "that we are one essential energy; and in the alpha state with senses activated, the infinite universe presents layers of manifestation for the third eye to envision. Duality exhibits a field of opposites which demands learning how to plant our desires for optimal affect. We can sense there is something more satisfying than what we have in this time-space frame, but how do we change the picture if we don't like it? How do we invite the realization of our fondest dreams of love, creative expression and prosperity?"

The angel replied, *What you resist persists. Let your self-righteousness dissipate into Love's transcendent redemption. The happiness of conscious discovery far outweighs the stagnation of ignorance. Life supportive action creates more love in the world, while following one's bliss honors the gift of free will. Use your imagination—imagine . . .*

So I imagined . . . the moon over a tropical ocean . . . my love and I on a swing . . . the sound of waves . . . a pungent smell of mango in the air . . . the taste of realized dreams.

And again the angel spoke, *Imagine . . . we are not creating things—we are Creation from which all things are coming.*

Do what fills your heart with joy.

BREATHE

Some mornings the ache is more hollow
like a womb after a still-born baby.
Medicate or meditate—
whatever it takes to feel alive.

I love the leafy green
outside my bedroom window.
Sun glints silver off leaves while
others shine bright, translucent green.

It reminds me of the day
I heard water sing, saw
sap blood run through leaf veins
and I was breathing with it.

It's hard living on the rainbow bridge;
footing gets unclear: Heaven? Earth?
The blend seems impossible,
but witches live between the worlds . . .

so I just breathe.

VIII
STRENGTH

I have what it takes . . .

+ **DIVINE FORCE • STRENGTH**

− **ABUSE OF POWER • WEAKNESS**

STRENGTH

My strength is within.

Choosing love over fear, I become the magnificence of which I am capable. Taming the wild inner beast requires awareness, perseverance, forgiveness, acceptance and healthy self love.

I release negative emotions, non-supportive thought patterns, and compulsive behaviors, no longer needing to give up my power to things. I know that as we perceive, we become.

Reforming erroneous thought and patterns that do not cultivate well-being takes application and commitment to practice. Strength means walking my talk and expressing myself truthfully, with love.

I am a vigilant observer
maintaining neutral witness
to effectively reprogram
habitual response.

I am strong in Spirit.

In My Studio

Foghorns would break the insomniac silence,
and I would paint—the action a loving blanket,
hands therapeutic the way a brush feels
as it reveals the story and all the
strength it takes to be.

He said we could live together, but—
music and meditation, and the recall
of what was said echoed the past
and all the lovers who had
harvested my garden.

They were in my room, critics all,
projecting their image for me to enact,
conditions to meet for love.
I had done it before,
acting a part, getting to play.

I had taken to heart every nuance of script
inspired to give my all to the king—
But this time I knew
I had transcended that place
and found it wanting.

Longing for the picture I'd like to see
seems to keep it away from me,
perfect health, money and mate.

What would I do to amplify
the vibration of peace?

A Prayer for Power

A fallen angel,
I have faltered
forgetting
I Am God/dess.

May I sing
a harmonic vibration,
and my power nurture
all beings as myself.

May I inspire joy,
transforming negativity
while expanding perspective,
with clarity and compassion.

May my whole being
reflect great beauty as a
healer and revealer of wisdom
who upholds a peaceful world.

IX
The Hermit

Ask one who knows . . .

+ ILLUMINATION • SELF KNOWLEDGE
~ OBJECTION • RESISTANCE

The Hermit

Light Bearer, show the way.

Listen, for I am the one who has gone before so that the way be made clear, and this I know . . .

A glimmer of light beckons us awake from darkness as the natural tendency toward a Greater Universal Principle ignites the desire to communicate with one's inner Self.

When we need to regroup, repair and return to our chosen path, we seek to reestablish our foundation through union with our Source energy. Turning to the positive, we utilize whatever works to establish unity.

Tools, teachers, rituals, practices and viable disciplines abound. The possibility of alignment with Cosmic Principle is unlimited, eternal and forever available for the asking.

Ask yourself: Am I shining my light?

Jai Guru Dev Maharishi

Joined with
Absolute
Infinity

Grace has emanated from
Universal consciousness
Realigning, redefining,
Unifying all parts.

Deep in
Eternity I Am
Verified, validated.

Multitudes of gratitude
Arise from the
Happiness of
Absolute
Reality
Inherent in the
Silence that is
Home for an
Infinite Self.

ELEMENTAL PEACE SONG

Fire, Water, Earth and Air,
every person everywhere,
Spirit knows our deepest prayer
for love to heal the world.

Fairies, fairies in the grove,
dancing, prancing on the ground,
as you circle, grant my wish
for peace the world around.

Angels, angels of the air,
spread a message hearts can hear,
so each will sing its fervent prayer
for peace around the world.

Sylphs, wood nymphs and water sprites,
nature's devas shine your light,
life affirming love's reward
for peace throughout the world.

People, people everywhere,
Fire, Water, Earth and Air,
come express your deepest prayer
for love to rule the world.

X
The Wheel Of Fortune

Round and round we go . . .

+ CHANGE +

- CHANGE −

The Wheel of Fortune

Be true to yourself and know freedom of spirit,
no matter the fortune—negative or positive.

From the well of Spirit, I create material wealth and give forth relative to the impassioned desire and visualization expressed.

I am Karma, the Law of Cause and Effect.

Aligning with the essential energy from which goodness emanates issues forth an invitation for a frictionless flow of abundance—

Know that when you act *as above, so below*, I manifest your vision with grace.

Are you ready to receive your good?

A Wheel Story

Raised to serve men, I believed
my fortune depended on them.
I did not envy the penis,
but the status and freedom
having one implied.

Though I vowed not to marry,
I did it three times—
the free love philanderer,
emotionally challenged genius,
and meditating physicist.

Each had charm enough to woo me,
to help me believe I mattered.
We shared high ideals:
the artist—the scientist—the guru,
heart—mind—spirit.

Fortune fluctuates
up—down—in—out
love—money.
The wish list is longer each day.

Three strikes and
you are out of the game,
yet I would still get up to bat
knowing that I have more to give,
loving each moment lived.

I do what I like and love when I do,
trusting the transit through illusion to see
there is nothing to own in the end,
and life itself appears on loan
as we ride the wheel.

Cycles

Cyclically changing acts
shapeshift our days
modify our nights
regulate experience
on the way
to all and
no
thing.

The journey from heart
to center each spoke
in concentric grace
circles infinity
on fortune's
winding path
to perfect
the gift.

XI

JUSTICE

Be fair . . .

+ EQUITY • JUSTICE • REASON

− BIAS • INJUSTICE

JUSTICE

*Mercy invites forgiveness, and compassion
generates richer rewards than strict justice.*

I, Justice, exemplify the application of Cosmic Law through human action.

How do you deal with challenges?

How do you maneuver circumstance?

Successful action reflects the mental state of agreement one has with things as they really are.

Discriminatory power combined with intuition develops practical life skills. Trust in a positive outcome attracts optimal solution; a conviction that everything is in cosmic order is life affirming.

I cut through illusion to discern the best, most fair course of action. A just life is more easily negotiated with clear knowledge of the actual situation, and with maintaining a grounded, balanced perspective.

4563

Four thousand
five hundred and
sixty-three mornings
at least
dawned with
the bed empty
like my arms.

Memories
amplify loneliness
and thousands
of restless nights
defy balance
as they harbor
yesterday.

In this twilight,
clarity permeates
the dark corners
of tomorrow
with hope—and
in between time,
I wait.

Shadows

She was in a dark light
waiting for the wind to change,
a sign that her heart
would not fail the task
of letting go the insistent past.

A peacock spread his tail
to win the hen with
impressive chatter; and
her smile betrayed the force
of his social intercourse.

With just enough movement
to change forever,
emerging from shadows,
demeanor resolved,
with life in hand,

She said . . .
I will not sacrifice myself
on Ego's altar,
but rather celebrate
the beauty we are.

Even in the deepest void,
I know you;
what you hide, I seek.
In your soul's closet,
we sit holding the key.

XII
The Hanged One

Let go . . .

+ RELEASE • SACRIFICE

− ATTACHMENT • BONDAGE

The Hanged One

We sacrifice to save . . .

I, The Hanged One, advise that we intuit our deepest heart rather than depend on ego-motivation. Align activity with Cosmic Law; cultivate Samadhi, a state of union with the divine; and know the consciousness of pure Being. Releasing old patterns and renouncing separation from Divinity enables the embrace and expression of our indwelling deified power.

Be willing to forfeit one thing to attain something better. A spiritual sacrifice involves devotion, service, worship and deferring to a Higher Power, your own True Self.

As you take responsibility for yourself, you set the stage for profound transformation through surrender. You gain a new perspective and are reborn, relinquishing that which no longer serves.

Vows once made, though betrayed, were never really broken. They remain threads woven into a forever tapestry of life, and somewhere in perpetuity, they are.

I forgive, and I release
to let _____ guide my life
a. divine love
b. pure light
c. higher Self
d. reason . . .
for I am One in Spirit
and there is only room for
Love.

We Take Them On

We
can rest
secure in the
knowledge that
when we take on
the meek or poor
to help, hinder, or
hide we're insecure,
we fill our space with
dependency to further need,
an ego's garden
choked with weeds.
Between empty and full,
heart's completion is the goal.
Fully realized, self-actualized,
liberated in the light of choosing love,
we
extend,
expand,
and overflow
with blessings
that humans know
in passage to unity.

All Souls' Hallowed Day

Holy Martyrs,
Ancestors,
Apostles,
Confessors,
All just and perfect servants
Who rest in Gaia's womb . . .
This is your hallowed day.

Today we feast abundance,
the harvest we celebrate,
and the long night before us.

We commemorate
the little
and grand deaths
that love demands
of Saints,
Angels,
and Elementals,
of those who soothe chaos
in the core of suffering.

Martyrs and givers of good,
heartfelt, we honor you—
resting our hidden selves
upon the altar
of our perception.

Spirits rise on this eve
to bid us listen . . .

"Here we are; remember us?
We are the lantern that never dims.
We stand certain that life itself
demands Spirit's kiss.
Each goodness grows more,
and each evil let go
engenders freedom."

So we are all
saints and martyrs
at choice for love.

The holy dance in fallen leaves
anticipating a dark season, with
harvest stored and hearth fires out.

In the sacred grove,
new fires are lit to share
warmth and plenty
for every home.

With martyrs honored
for their virtue,
and saints their
souls fulfilled,
the dead rest settled,
their graves adorned
with fruit—

And we
honor ourselves every day
that we sacrifice ego
to propagate Truth.

North Invocation

We call upon the North Spirit,
Mother Gaia, who teaches the
value of being grounded,
nurturing the fertile seed,
and fulfilling valid need.

Abuk, Ala, Oshun, Ymaya,
Isis, Bast, Beset, and the Hathors,
Ariadne, Cybele, Demeter, Hera,
Hestia, Leda, Rhea, Rumia Dea,
Aditya, Devi, Indrani, Tara, Yoni,
Mama Paccha, Xi Wang Mu,
White Buffalo Calf Woman,
Sussistannako, Estsan Atlehi,
Arianrhod, Brigid, Danu,
Gwenhwyfar, Maga, Mórrigán,
Mary, and all the names
that are You,

We call upon the North Spirit
with benediction and praise
to bless us with
wisdom.

Blessed,
Be.

North

Earth ♦ Pentacles
Physical ♦ Wisdom
Sacrifice ♦ Result

Sometimes I Wonder Why . . .

I laugh
when
I should not,
mirrored
beside myself,
ice melting
into
Spring.

My heart
releases
its regrets,
wings on wind,
leaves
leaving.

XIII

TRANSITION

This too will pass . . .

+ COMPLETE CHANGE • REBIRTH

− INERTIA • STAGNATION

TRANSITION

From caterpillar to butterfly . . .

I, Transition, am ruled by the fixed astrological water sign Scorpio whose energy is intense—powerful, vital, desirous, forceful, creative, transforming and resourceful. Employing this energy through authentic or Higher Self-functioning allows one to apply creative resourcefulness to transform adversity and invite renewal.

Death whispers:

"Remember to fully embrace life,
One Source, One Light, One Life Energy.

Dying to some thing
encourages and promotes
genesis and reform.

Choose to view loss
as an opportunity
to gain a higher,
more enlightened
perspective.

The natural
motion of death,
transformation
and rebirth
uplifts
your soul.

The Deer

When I close my eyes,
the scene plays again—
a beautiful deer in the center road
confused . . .
and the truck with its long flatbed
passing the deer unseen,
driving on unaware
of the parts left behind.

Red flew by so fast
the doe had no time to suffer . . .
small blessing.

My daughter's "NO!"
broke the air like gunshot
as we held each other hard,
tears for the deer,
and the sad fact
that life is mortal.

I thought
how fortunate we were . . .
What if the deer
had chosen my car?
Belly tight,
trauma released slowly,

And I gratefully
treasured
life's fleeting
moment.

Eight A.M.

Angels welcomed a
Great woman with
Anthems of praise as
They carried her into
Heaven, wrapped in
Absolute surrender.

During meditation,
she spoke to me
saying her body
was too weak;
and I agreed—

like a dried chrysalis,
and she was ready to fly.

I saw her globe of light,
exultant, no age, all ages,
vibrating wings of radiant
energy waves.

She was in the desert,
and I the mountains,
when she left the
dried shell that had
housed her 77 years.

I checked the clock: 8:00—
the call came at 9:00
that she passed at 8:00 A.M.

XIV

Temperance

Take it easy.

+ MODERATION • PATIENCE • VERIFICATION

− BURN-OUT • DISCORD • EXCESS

Temperance

From lead, gold . . .

The art of tempering concerns making a properly balanced mixture. I, Temperance, integrate opposites uniting Spirit and matter. By moderating extremes, I achieve equanimity. Temper, or maturation, is tested by daily challenge.

Souls invite their trials to benefit a transformation of personality, expanding consciousness. Balance is necessary to clearly perceive the universal principles and laws by which life operates.

The goal of enlightenment is realized when the human personality, the microcosm, aligns with Deity, the macrocosm. Through listening to and employing divine guidance, the Higher Self evolves.

Personal refinement results automatically with the realization of Source Essence. Alignment harmonizes, integrates and makes whole the various components of human personality.

Grand Cross

Conceived in passion, my baby daughter did not smile for over a month; and then, it could have been colic. With parents torn between love and war, she felt battle bruised, even though we professed our love.

When Daddy left, she ached for years. The stepdad I chose was like ice for her after a tropical storm—no more emotion, just behave.

She was gifted a mouse, a bird, her own room . . . and her first taste of longing for the daddy that never really was.

Trees outside the bedroom window sang of seasons with pink, green, gold, brown and decay. Her life reflected change as myriad scenes expressed drama, comedy, and the ever present hope to integrate the two.

Astrology confirmed all four corners of her life crossed, a grand opportunity to overcome adversity . . . yet at times so dark, tears could not fall.

Meeting the challenge, she would gain the stature of her unlimited power. Contemplating this, she thought:

The window light breaks half shadow, half bright. I walk between, a thin line down the middle. This ribboned tributary boomerangs back, smiles for anyone who dares deep love. Transcending the confines of projected sight, maintaining an oceanic view forgives a darkly placid sea, illumining the moments of the Self I want to be.

The Visionary

I am like
a worm churning earth,
digging for millions of years,
ancient patterns etched on walls.

A worm forever,
how could there be anything
but the next bit of dirt?

I have a mind
to crawl my way out
bite by bite.

It is hard transforming
from worm to wo/man,
from chains to choice.

There is comfort in moving soil;
but I will overcome this
earthbound crucible;
and I will ascend the stars.

XV
The Deceiver

Snake said, "I am really a rope."

+ MATERIAL ATTACHMENT • DECEPTION
- RELEASE FROM BONDAGE

The Deceiver

Deception often masquerades as beauty.

I, The Deceiver, am the coyote who teaches life's lessons through chaos and trickery. Error occurs when decisions are motivated by fear. Lies, role-playing, showing off, superficiality and vanity are the result of insecurity.

The enemy is fear; the solution is trust in your divinity, knowing and choosing truth, making decisions based on facts, rather than perceptual projection.

Temptation may suggest you do something for money that offends your soul, or to manipulate people and circumstances for selfish gain.

You can refuse to misuse your personal power.

See through illusion as you gain spiritual understanding and liberation. Functioning from your divine Self indicates that wisdom has been gained relative to greed and possessiveness.

Your illumined spirit celebrates the release of bondage, free to fulfill your fondest heart's desire.

Dancing with the Demon

He was frightfully handsome,
a charismatic magnet
smart women would avoid.
He seemed to fathom
dark secrets before I did,
found them in my attic,
stroked them alive.

Down tunnels of
forgetfulness,
lost in sensual abuse,
regret's refuse longed for
the life I knew before
the wolf bayed my door.

Later, I faced the dark moon,
befriended my mirror,
and danced . . .

Memories crowded my
psyche, recalling how
it felt before his agitation
sent every cell screaming,
when order prevailed.

In Pandora's box, only hope
remained after years of confusion,
layers of missions and remissions,
and belief in a calling—

so I danced.

A Bard in the Bardo

Projecting, correcting,
words get sticky
binding God to concept,
elusive and distant.

Luck makes victims for sure,
yet field lilies are swaying
the breeze once more,
secure in their beauty.

Again, a thought of him
twenty years after the fall
and the phone rang
singing his name—

There was no one there,
a buzz, an out of order reply
to "I'll always love you"
vowed long ago.

The day I walked away
changed my life forever.

XVI
The Tower

It's gone too far. . .

+ Cosmic Direction

− Stagnation • Entrapment

The Tower

An ending is an opportunity to begin again.

I, The Tower, represent divine cosmic direction that transmutes corrupted perspective and releases the error that separated one temporarily from one's fundamental Source. Enlightenment occurs as the Law of Cause and Effect intervenes to set life straight.

Reassessing one's life and belief systems initiates rapid change. Welcome the opportunity to see things as they really are, for denying an issue shocks the system when awareness reveals.

Relax your nerves—bath soak, nature walk, meditate, soothe your soul and be good to yourself.

Revelation brings positive change for the better, for you are no longer imprisoned by ignorance.

Know this and be liberated.

At the Window

She set her rocker by the window
for moments of contemplation.

The garden reflected her moon and
the phases of mood that emotion plays.

Spring had bud, then Summer's bloom;
now, Autumn's leaves were turning.

They smelled of mulch and the musk
of age that drenched her attic clothes.

As she rocked, she breathed the garden
thinking, *After Winter's frost, Spring*.

Mystery

I AM
the
Miracle
You
Seek
Through the
Enlightened
Reflection of
Your Self.

XVII

The Star

Shine . . .

+ Hope • Inspiration • Optimism

− Disappointment • Pessimism

The Star

Express your stellar magnificence.

I, The Star, representing the Law of Luminosity, invite you to shine as an individual expression of Cosmic Mind. All wisdom resides in the universal subconscious for you to cognize.

Established in Being, one experiences a frictionless flow of evolution. Promised the future accomplishment of present goals, you can accept your good and realize your desires.

Recognize the star you are, and self-esteem increases. The more confidence, the more you achieve and embrace your vision with enthusiasm and dedication.

Contemplate yourself surrounded by that which you intend. See, be and express your brilliance.

What we deem supernatural phenomena is naturally ordinary within the context of itself, so be true to yourself and shine.

SHINING

This poem is for you
who are brightly shining
through the bars of your
pining for freedom.

The sound of your name
resounds with the flair
of thousands who
answer the same.

Yet no one except you
can be as you are—
genuine, unique,
a brilliant star,

And this poem
I have written
is just for
you.

Love

I have loved you
>In thunder storms and quiet days,
>In ocean waves on windy shores,
>In light, dark, breath and death,
>>Energy remains.

I smell you
>Musk honey melon ripe,
>Incense-rich velvety skin,
>Every sense alert, alive, enlivened.
>>Anticipation gains.

I taste you
>Upon my lips;
>Skin shivers with longing,
>The yearning in itself complete.
>>Synergy reigns.

I hear you
>Within a subtler self
>That knows beyond the words we say,
>Because of all the worlds we weave,
>>Innocence ordains.

I see you
>In every blade of grass
>Or sand grain beneath the sea;
>Invisible movement views us
>>As Spirit once again.

We touch
>Mergers of divine embrace,
>One love feels expanded
>Two times two to the tenth and more,
>>Beyond measure.

BEDAZZLED

Bedazzled, tingled, energized—
One by one, dreams pass by.
Illusions of a subtle ilk,
like silken threads entangle.

Fortunes rise and fall;
lovers come and go.
Our fondest attachments
imprison our souls.

What then?

Tendrils of delusion dissolve
with a promise to set us free
and release the stellar Self,
the One we were meant to Be.

My Goddess

A blueprint, a prototype—one of a kind,
her exquisite body houses a beautiful mind,
a heart so pure, her love flows in harmony.

Had I met her in my youth,
I would have been intimidated.
I would have judged her journey,
questioned her wisdom,
discarded her truth
for a perception,
a belief.

Even now I doubt, which
clouds my gait with insecurity.
My wheel turns the more I crave.

In a sacred circle weaving spirals,
ever ascending, ever descending,
the ebb flows, decays, grows . . .

I spin right, left, catch the wind,
ride it for all I'm worth, sink or swim
on a life dive, trusting my silent voice.

I knew my goddess when a child—
just a feeling, a sense, a simply being.
I could listen for lifetimes to her song.

EAST

Air ♦ Swords
Intellect ♦ Enlightenment
Consciousness ♦ Opportunity

Faerie Night

Angels, elves and things,
as faerie night begins,
circle in forest groves
where silver bells ring,
calling in twilight.

The indigo hue bids
each a task to bear—
angels to the human realm,
elves to tend the forest,
faeries to the air.

Owls, night birds and bats
secretly dart through trees,
creatures rarely seen
living in the shadows,
populating dreams.

XVIII
The Moon

See with intuition . . .

+ ILLUSION • INTUITION
- MINOR DECEPTION

The Moon

Trust yourself to know . . .

My cyclic nature transits from new moon to full, with gently consistent rotation. Reflecting the Sun, I experience smooth evolutionary change in which a cycle's end heralds new beginnings.

However, my fluctuation can bring unexpected occurrence, inviting the discovery of subconscious influences, motivations and stirring emotions. This presents the option to get real, face oneself, and liberate from ego's deception—imposed or self-inflicted.

My Piscean psychic energy may inspire a dream or vision to which wishful thinking could attach. One often connects ideas to happenings that can block other points of view when there is more yet to be revealed.

Combining objective witness with one's deepest intuitive voice reveals what is true.

The embodiment of honest love and caring moves one beyond deception—Trust in your ability to perceive illusion and live a more conscious life.

Though Miles Apart

You bathed me last night with
telepathic moments of moonlight.
You moved in with grace
and licked my tears.

I depend on your compassion;
warmth heals pain,
feeds a hunger of lifetimes,
centers the soul.

Days disappear down
alleys of forgetfulness.
Threads of love unite them,
one continuum, always changing.

Since we parted,
I have felt your presence.
Should we not speak again,
I still know you.

I have seen the light that
glows your nobility;
I have felt your
heart shine.

REACHING . . .

Sentient tentacles oscillate
in an ocean of thought,
sensing every wave—

repeated scenes of
love, death, violence
and ultimate surrender.

Through countless tributaries
of desire, buds blossom,
wither, drop seeds,

reaching for the sun.

XIX
The Sun

Be happy!

+ Attainment • Golden Opportunity • Joy

- Poverty of Spirit • Unhappiness

The Sun

Yes, joy and happiness are yours.

Radiate your light as do I, The Sun. Be powerful, influential, magnetic, enjoying a victorious life of success.

Life force enlivens an alert mind with a sunny disposition, a soaring spirit, and the ability to grow fortune . . . health, romance, well-being—the fulfillment of desire.

Self-reliant, trusting and joyful, you feel secure, protected, and loved. Favorable circumstances prevail.

Clouds do disperse . . .

Fulfillment is your birthright.

Bright Spot

Centered heart's radius
3.14159265 . . . Perfect Pi,
the bright spot,
clear light,
love . . .

We
are suns,
radiant suns
recreating suns,
populating galaxies,
expanding the universe.

Enlightened, our silent name
sparks creation with only
a smile for perfection,
igniting laughter
in full circle
radiant
suns.

CHRIST LIGHT

It was so hot you could fry an egg on pavement;
and the heat lay oppressive on my lungs.

Between wake and sleep, I envisioned eyes
of pure love, feeling total acceptance.

I was suddenly home, no doubt, no fear,
inspired by Guides to guidance . . .

We have so much to give you;
you just have to get out of the way.

Bright pictures of Christ and the light pouring
forth through clouds, or the hands of God . . .

I was moved . . . *Shine brighter the more you give,*
and receive without attachment.

Give all concern to me that I may reside
in grace within a willing heart.

Should you forget that we are one being, I will
wait silent for you to hear our refrain again.

No matter the challenge, I do listen
sooner or later . . . and I come Home.

XX
JUDGMENT

When one finger points, three point back.

+ ATONEMENT • SELF-ANALYSIS

− INDECISION • CRITICISM • SELF-DENIAL

JUDGMENT

Judge not, that ye be not judged . . .
—Mathew 7:1, Holy Bible

I, the representative of atonement, suggest you forgive that which does not renew Spirit so that life will flow more favorably. Spiritual evolution naturally results in an enlightened universal consciousness.

Critical judgment tends to separate us from ourselves and others. Deliverance occurs from releasing attachments or attitudes that have held us back. Conscious discrimination protects against victimization, manipulation and domination from non-supportive people or concepts.

Increased awareness and the right use of personal power dissolve what blocks your True Self expression. Maintain integrity to live in alignment with Divine Will, sourcing unlimited energy and potentials, empowered and displaying moral excellence.

Change is inevitable;
fear blocks progress.
Follow your conscience
consciously.

To Be or Not

The initial question suggests life's ebb
flows according to will.

Each thought-created drama turns
the karmic wheel toward Home.

Why the show? The suffering? Meaning?
When and how can we know Peace?

Round and round the thinker goes
until silence accepts itself.

However we perceive the matrix,
we are blessed with connection.

Are you joyous beyond happy? Have you
asked lately if you are really alive?

We get lost in thought and activity,
future projected and past reflected.

Where are you now?

On Awaking: Gratitude

The grey dawn slowly brightened
with strands of sun
breaking through blinds
streaming across the bed, onto
the still cold from night floor.

Life felt distant, like
having hibernated through
a long, dark winter
deep in the snow of slumber
longing to laugh.

And black was soothing,
a loving blanket that
wrapped warm the soul,
getting past months of bed rest
and wanting to run.

The light demands action,
days dreaming blossom
and a harvest of love—
the health of body,
mind, spirit and soul.

Of course there is suffering.
Experience is a journey for
the witness to embrace, yet
that for which we are grateful
far outweighs the challenge.

XXI
The Universe

I have arrived . . . again.

+ Completion • Fulfillment • Synthesis

− Imperfection • Stagnation

The Universe

I am That I Am.

Self-actualized, victorious and expressive of pure Love, I enjoy the play and display of life's expression, and am triumphant in all endeavor.

Having mastered the limitations of material existence, I gratefully receive my heart's desire.

Self-acceptance breeds self-respect and reverence toward all sentient beings, as well as appreciation for all creation. Fully aware of who I really am, I take responsibility for expressing and realizing my potential.

Now is the time to embrace my Self—being responsible and employing the administrative duties for my personal universe to invite success.

Choosing to live in love, doing harm to none, life flows harmoniously for I am aligned with my authentic, divine nature.

Nectar

Felt to the bone, it
appeared unannounced,
crept in like fog,
dispersed like rain.

I waited for years
to feel it,
taste the nectar,
make the vision real.

Why resist the eternal
flow of emergence,
the abundant gift of
thought, desire, form?

A forever pregnant
womb of potential
motivates my soul
to believe.

ELEMENTAL RITUAL

On the wheel of my altar,
I place Fire in the South
to purify and release
attachment.

In the West, Water,
to flow with Nature and
know my deepest Self
to be oceanic Love.

I place flowers in the North
with a prayer for fulfillment,
the dream to manifest
Heaven on Earth.

In the East, feathers
to lift my soul and soar
with Spirit, accepting
the gift that I Am.

In the Center, I stand firm;
Sun, Dolphin, Eagle, Oak,
Fire, Water, Air, Earth, I am
thankful for elemental grace.

CENTER

All ♦ Nothing
Sythesis ♦ Completion
Fulfillment ♦ True Self

PRESENT
Now
Be
Be
Now
Present

At Hilltop Ranch

In gratitude for John and Bonnie Gray

I needed to find *the right spot*.
What that meant was obscure
as I hiked camera in hand,
an artist seeking eternity,
in love with nature,
sounds, colors.

Sensing gateways, I saw
three convergent paths
in a grove of redwoods.
It was mine; I knew it—
and marked the spot with
twigs forming a six-pointed star.

Then energy flooded my veins
and traversed my spine;
with arms raising in surrender.
It was a crucifixion, a calling,
a clearing, a cleansing . . .
Embodying nature, I prayed.

I realized the first path
from which I entered
was the past,
the second now, and
the third an uphill climb
to what might be.

There was a significant fourth,
but it was a way not taken.

The grove filled with song:
a woodpecker, bees, birds,
mosquito, wind rustling,
yet I was deeply silent.

And I heard,
Feel the love of Mother;
Her womb of life
incubates desire
and heals that which
fails Creation.

Power abused grows fear;
but that is not true love.
Be not afraid of
Father's judgment—
It defines, discriminates, and
sets conditions for love to grow.

Tears fell like a wash after rain
and the sun rose inside me . . .
I felt wholly loved, knowing
that woman is desire and man
the energy to act on it—
and that I am both.

What that means is yet unknown,
but there is still an uphill climb
and more to discover.

Epilogue

The world is the stage upon which we act.

Perception from beginning to completion is an objective linear concept conceived to understand a subjective experience. It is logical to view our walk on planet Earth from birth to death because we are living an obvious sequence.

Whether we believe in reincarnation or not, the personality we wear now is all there is in this incarnation. No matter how many billion human beings and quadrillion other species inhabit this orb, we are each a unique life-form with specific DNA.

Apparently separate, we share similar challenges, have kindred responses, emotions, thoughts and ways of acting out. We act according to our conscience, and our choices are based on our degree of awareness.

As we circumambulate the karmic wheel, we begin and end many times in one lifetime, accumulating stories and attitudes throughout, acting many parts. The stages of human development—infancy, childhood, youth, adult, middle-age, senior and old-age—each have their wisdom to impart.

Maps of consciousness serve as ambassadors of wisdom; and there are numerous representations that chart a course to enlightenment. We acquire the treasure Tarot offers by embodying the principles inherent in its 22 Major Arcana archetypes.

The passage from Fool to Universe, like the evident stages of life, appears linear. However, any one of the archetypes could occur at any age. We are continuously integrating information, digesting what we receive, and projecting our perceptions.

Consider that one's journey is a collection of stories the objective self can observe and interpret to make meaning out of life. Mastering life requires the integration of both objective (yang) and subjective (yin) energies, thus unifying mental and spiritual aspects of personality.

We write our scripts, direct our plays, and reap what we sow. Eventually, we surrender to a higher power, something beyond mortality.

I invite you to assess the scenes you have acted out relative to Tarot's 22 Major Arcana. What archetype(s) did that part of your life invoke? What lessons were present and wisdom gained?

We are free to make this life what we want; how we respond to daily challenges and circumstance is our choice. The Law of Attraction can attract love or war, and what we think and feel creates our world.

Again, I thank Reverend Agatha for her profound and awakening statement heard hundreds of times before integration:

It is your own picture show.

Here's to a successful play and a long run!

I have shared my mind; perhaps it spoke to you.

Welcome always to my heart
with a prayer for Peace.

Melanie

The 22 Major Arcana Archetypes

SOUTH: *Fire, Purification*

0 The Fool: *Innocence*
at choice, willing to take a leap of faith, learning from one's actions

I The Magus: *Individuality*
mastering ego, manifesting from above below

II The High Priestess: *Subconsciousness*
revealing hidden wisdom, accessing the Void

III The Empress: *Fertile Abundance*
the feminine or yin aspect of self, the incubating womb of desire

IV The Emperor: *Powerful Authority*
the masculine or yang aspect of self, the active principle

V The Hierophant: *Tradition*
dogma, religious ideals, honoring tradition with an open mind

VI The Lovers: *Love*
trust, harmonious choice, the balance of yin and yang

WEST: *Water, Introspection*

VII The Chariot: *Victorious Control*
right action

VIII Strength: *Courage*
Higher Self functioning over ego force, love over fear

IX The Hermit: *Enlightened Self Knowledge*
reflecting the light of spiritual attainment

X The Wheel of Fortune: *Change*
cycles, fluctuating circumstance, acquiring flexibility

XI Justice: *Equilibrium*
fairness, reason, maintaining inner and outer balance
XII The Hanged One: *Sacrifice*
letting go that which does not serve to uphold creation,
changing priorities

NORTH: *EARTH, WISDOM*

XIII Transition: *Complete Change*
death and rebirth
XIV Temperance: *Moderation*
patience, alchemically transforming negative to positive
energy, balance
XV The Deceiver: *Material Attachment*
fear, bondage of spirit, overcoming addictive behaviors
and habits
XVI The Tower: *Cosmic Direction*
awakening, facing oneself
XVII The Star: *Inspiration*
hope, optimism, meditation, achieving goals

EAST: *AIR, ENLIGHTENMENT*

XVIII The Moon: *Illusion*
dreams, developing intuition
XIX The Sun: *Attainment*
golden opportunity, embracing joy
XX Judgment: *Atonement*
self-analysis, self-acceptance
XXI The Universe: *Completion*
fulfillment, self actualized

WE ARE . . .

This thought
Has set me free:

We are the hands,
That express Divine Mind.

About the Artist-Author

Living artfully, with integrity, guides my life.
I seek to express Truth in personal vision,
to communicate honestly with consideration,
committed to excellence in all endeavor.
I choose to be authentic.
—Melanie Gendron

Born in Boston, MA, Melanie attended The School of the Museum of Fine Arts, Boston in affiliation with Tufts University.

She has developed a unique style rich in symbolism inspired by many cultures. Proficient in a variety of media, Melanie enjoys a renaissance attitude, creating with inspiration her authentic expression of Spirit. Melanie's prize winning artwork is widely exhibited and represented in numerous collections, both public and private.

Among her publications are the internationally acclaimed *Gendron Tarot, A Journal for Cat Lovers* and *The Goddess Remembered, a Spiritual Journal.*

Melanie is a multimedia, multi-tasking, professional artist who has served a variety of clients as: animator, art director, author, book designer, fashion designer, graphic artist, illustrator, poet, painter, portraitist, teacher—metaphysician, intuitive counselor—whatever skill applies to give her best effort.

She currently manages Gendron Studios in the Santa Cruz Mountains of California, offering fine and commercial art and tarot products and services, on the web at www. melaniegendron.com, Email gentarot@comcast.net.

Also By Melanie Gendron

The Gendron Tarot, deck and book, ©1997 & 2004,
U.S. Games Systems, Inc.

The Goddess Remembered, A Spiritual Journal, ©1990,
Crossing Press

A Journal for Cat Lovers, ©1990,
Crossing Press

Contained by a cohesive vision, Melanie Gendron partitions her poetically painted rooms, housed in *This Fool's Journey.* Cleverly calling upon the elemental spirits, she spins cycles in duality's direction, the four corners of life: North and South, East and West, instilled inside our Center. As she shares each Arcana from her personally insightful journey, she weaves hidden names and messages within the patterns of our lives, moving emotions overflowing our empty cup. Melanie Gendron 'geminizes' words with dual meanings, unfolding archetypal visions released to channel the enlightenment of self-actualization and free will through her penetrating poetry. So, "Breathe" in "Shadows" of Pandora's Box while "Dancing with the Demon," "Reaching . . ." "Though Miles Apart," the senses from the "Love" of "My Goddess."

—Justin R. Hart, Poetic Author of *Harmonic Hart Visions of Goddesses, Angel, Mermaids, and Fairy Tales* and *The Crystal Kaleidoscope of a Searching Silhouette*
www.harmonic-hart-visions.com

Printed in the United States of America

www.ingramcontent.com/pod-product-compliance
Lightning Source LLC
Chambersburg PA
CBHW031859090426
42741CB00005B/563